Toward a Personal Psychology

By
Martin Hersey

Toward a Personal Psychology

AN INNER MONOLOGUE

Dedicated to
Donna Cotzen, M.D.

Written between
2004-2007

Part I

Words are not sufficient. How do you express experience?
No matter what it is, it all runs out in the end.
The results of therapy come out after the actual therapy hour.
All my life, they stopped me from getting what I wanted. Now I
don't know anymore.
A lot of life is about knowing when to talk and when to listen.
My mind works a certain way--I can't change that, but I can change
what's in it.
I don't expect to ever get well. Intensive therapy only makes me
worse.
I have suppressed personality syndrome or SPS.
I have hallucinatory persecutory complex or HPC.
I have repetitive thinking syndrome or RTS.
Mental patient stigma--Your thoughts are worthless because you
are mentally ill.
Some things show themselves. Most of them don't--They remain
veiled.

Part I

If I could understand what is happening to me, I'd be a lot happier.
It's all so random and arbitrary. I fail to see the connections.
I hang on each day by the thread of reason.
I create these voices that talk to me all day. I will continue to use
them and be used by them until I no longer need them. I'm talking
to them. They are talking to me.
Maybe my consciousness is now in my speaking. I just don't
know what has taken over. Maybe it's a response to this noisy
environment. My right ear is plugged up.
My mind is like a bad child that never does what you tell it to do.
Whatever it is I think I am doing, I wish I would tell myself what it
is.
My rational mind can't understand my illness, but I _can_ dismantle it.
I'm the guy everyone talks to, but they don't know it.
I'm the most disconcerted guy in the state of New Jersey.
You're reduced to nothing by what? Your own thinking.
I'm the man who loved women who didn't love him.
When I was younger, I was wrong--So was everyone else. Now I'm
right and everyone else is wrong.
Words generate actions. Actions generate words.
At home, I talk to myself for hours. I am desperately in need of
someone to talk to.
Psychiatrists are benevolent, ignorant torturers.
I'm waiting for some woman. I've given up looking for her. I'm just
waiting.

Part I

Being well was not being able to think clearly. It was more like
being able to do something in the world.
This is too much consciousness for one man.
The better part of my nature is disturbed.
Man's limit of understanding himself is limited itself.
The well side is looking on while the ill side is parading about.
I am living life with some intensity but without purpose.
This is all something primitive. My thinking degenerates into idiocy.
 Occasional descents into idiocy. The house is an asylum.
It's as if a button is pushed in my unconscious, or someone forgot to
close a door. I can't control it, and I can't turn it off.
This stuff is all outside of me, and yet, it's coming from inside of
me. I can't know it(the stuff).
If the insane voices continue, I will no longer be able to think.
I'm getting sicker. Long periods of the day when I am taken over by
voices.
Recently, I have lost the capacity to reason. The only way I can
stay lucid is to talk aloud.
My thought patterns are all different from day to day.
A voice is louder than my thinking.

Part I

I'm embarrassed by and ashamed of other people, including my
therapist.
My mind emptied itself of its contents and stripped itself of its
personality. It split into various versions of itself.
Gonna the psychiatrist--liberality.
I'm struggling, just to make known to myself my own thoughts.
Part of the insanity is that you don't know what you are thinking.
My outside is good and well. My inside is all screwed up.
Too many reasons. Not enough reason.
My stability in the progression of the illness--maintaining it in spite
of an increase in my symptoms.
Reason is not just thinking correctly. It's doing correctly.
I'm now living on a subsistence level.
I'm nothing but a stomach.

Part I

My mind admits so many possibilities--there's little chance to act.
My conscious mind can't tell my unconscious mind to do anything.
Sound falls into silence so quickly.
Therapy with Gonna gave me insight into a woman and her
professionalism.
The truth of the matter is--it's your body against your mind.
My sexual misadventure has been absolutely debilitating.
I was not sufficiently developed as a person to be a parent after my
child reached her teen years.
My unconscious turns everything out mechanically.
Gonna was just not asserting herself to my liking.
We are acceding to reality all the time.
The situation here is and has been for quite some time, me without
the other.
I'm talking to myself--I'm not making any sense to anyone.
I have something with other people. They don't have anything with
me.
I can say--There's an enormous amount of change in my world from
day to day.
Do I miss these people? Or, what is it? No--I want to use their
names to my advantage.
I have learned I can manipulate my mind--but not without
repercussions.
There is nothing worse than a rebellious adult.
I've been insane all day--a big setback.
I was a classy extrovert when this stuff started. Now I'm nothing
at all.
It was me and Gonna for awhile. Then she just took over.
My insane man's voice is much simpler than that of the sane man. It
is beneath stupid and close to idiocy.
I express my displeasure with the world by withdrawing.
I couldn't see why Gonna wouldn't play along. She became so
serious.

Part I

I'm not satisfied with this version of reality I'm getting. I should
be getting a more real version of reality.
My mind is a mind that has gone awry due to psychotherapy and
psychoanalysis.
What will I do? I can't find food that I like anywhere.
I don't know what to do about them--the doctors--They act as if
they own the store. The patient is not important to them.
The curse of my sexuality.
I've completely dried up in this place. There's nothing here.
My inner world--the imagery--is all in black and white, not color.
None of this has any effect on me. I don't remember anything from
sentence to sentence. I live almost completely in the present.
I can see myself. I _do_ hear myself.
I don't see how to make another person act. It's hard to see how to
make myself act.
I can't find sufficient cause for my thoughts. I act unknowingly. I
have been a victim of objects.

Part I

There are two kinds of people--those with values, and those without values.
I want an end to boredom.
I didn't get what I wanted in life. Now it has all run out.
Treatment by psychiatrists has tended to infantilize me.
It's getting so I can't go out in public.
Society has totally abandoned me to myself.
I can't access a lot of what I'm experiencing mentally. Much of it has no meaning.
Excessive smoking, obsession with sex, isolation from other people, boredom.
I make innocent analogies with things which are taken by me as foolishness later on.
Desire rises and falls, finds some object to attach to.
I don't have good reasons for doing anything today.
You can't put a glove on consciousness--It's elusive and illusory.
I might be a man for somebody else's reason--This makes me less of a man.
When I close my eyes, I see degraded pictures--patchy grass, raggedy flowers. The quality of the images is poor.
I guess I could ask for what I want, but, for some reason, this usually backfires.
I can see I'm still rebelling--from what I don't know--myself I guess.
I can't find the right word (old age).
I've made my life's project myself--What are people going to think of me?
What will I do--What do I do--with this man I've made with therapy?
A perfect day--No disruption in my emotions.
In the world, it doesn't matter who you are. It's who you're taken for.
It's too bad I had to waste a whole life just to get to old age.

Part I

These days are worthless, rotten, and scary.
I say this is a malady of the old--to mean nothing.
I'm so tired of thinking, I can't think anymore.
Everything is so irrational and out of control--in a small way.
Malignant Therapy Syndrome--The patient overdoses on therapy.
He can't stop talking, even though the therapist is not there. (This
is not a joke. It has happened to me.)
All the attempts at explaining the world today are not working.
My insanity has a mind of its own, with its own vocabulary, grammar,
and syntax.
I'm always one step behind everyone else. Either I don't have a job
or that I'm a schizophrenic.
I falter without encouragement.
My brain is the driving force behind my mind.
My voices come out of my brain.
My rhythmic thinking goes on all day. Sometimes the channel is
changed.
Insane thinking draws wrong conclusions from wrong premises.
You don't have any effect on someone simply by thinking.
A man left alone, to his own devices, will inevitably fail.
Ideal images reside in, and are produced by, the Unconscious.
I've completely lost all measure of what passes for thinking.
I have been under Gonna's power. It is not a good relationship.

Part I

I can't find anything in here--I mean in my mind--It's all ideas.
Everything is a passivity.
You can never determine anything <u>without</u> thinking. You can never
determine anything <u>with</u> thinking.
Computers give a certain rarefied being that nothing else gives.
Fantasy--a spinoff of desire.
I have no answer for this--the riddle of consciousness.
I'm separated from my own experience. I don't see it through my
own eyes.
These sentences aren't consistent. They have not been. Only some
of them are.
Yesterday--all day long--a stream of insanity.
Something passive has taken over. My mind is being thought.
I was resentful at everything my therapist said to me. I had a bad
attitude toward her.
Not <u>what</u> I see, but what I <u>want</u> to see.
All these words are an innocent, repeating cycle of nonsense.
Mr-Know-It-All. Mr-Supposed-To-Be.
In my mind, there's no cause and effect any more. There's just
effect.
It's impossible to begin anywhere--It's already all gone.
The media are a garbage dump of words.
I can't do anything <u>with</u> other people. I can't do anything <u>without</u>
other people. So--I don't do anything.
The world seems plunged in darkness.
I had been waiting for a friend. There was Don, Marae.

Part I

I am a stubborn, willful obstinacy.
I'm talking from a point of view that has no validity in the world today.
An unheard voice--my voice.
I'm led to believe there is an inner world which is not accessible to the outer world, and an outer world which _is_ accessible to the inner world.
My mind is treacherous, betraying me at those times I want something from my perceptions.
My reasons for falling into insanity: boredom, missing another, having nothing to do.
I've grown tired of trying to help myself.
The changeable nature of my reality from day to day.
I have had some time to correct myself.
I must have my wires crossed in my brain--I am not making the proper connections.
I want more--I don't get more. I don't _do_ anything.
If all this is my mind, what am _I_ doing in it?
For the last week, unfortunately, knowing is gone.
Old Age: white hair, teeth, eyes, ears, digestion, skin, muscles; weak, soft body; sleep, mind.
I have no resources here--no professionals, no reliable people. It's the dead area--The Dead Zone.
An adult does not play tricks on himself.
There's nothing but cigarettes, gasoline, and groceries. I'm holed up here, defending this insanity I don't want.
I'm wrecking everything. It's envy--envy of one from Below of one Up Above.
I'm so proud of the things I've learned here, but the knowledge is so quickly and easily eroded.
I became an adult at 62. I also discovered I was mentally ill.
I am in search of uncertain truth.

Part I

Your mind knows all about you. You don't know it and it never tells
you.
I don't really experience my experience.
Comes the light of day, guilty creatures scurry away. Comes the
light of day, creatures who are guilty must scurry away.
Fantasy to the older person is nothing. It's an offshoot of their
mind the way it used to be.
The great whore--psychiatry.
I don't attempt a mind. Nor do I attempt a body. So, what am I?
In the hierarchy of merit that is society, I am usually near the
bottom.
I'm chasing my mind around in here. I can't find anything.

Part I

Now I can neither think nor not think, with the voices going on inside, and me speaking out loud.
It's the classic case of neglect--They don't want to have anything to do with me.
I noticed today the absolute irrelevancy of everything I'm doing.
I have my own version of reality, but no one partakes of it.
The power of my mind to deceive itself is extraordinary.
What I'm <u>supposed</u> to know and what I <u>do</u> know are two different things.
There's always something funny going on in here that is not me.
You have to keep ahead of your mind because it gets ahead of you.
My inner eye is not looking at anything real. It's moving about over things fantastic.
Reasons for falling into insanity--Boredom; Having nothing to do; Having no one.
Something perverse about a woman doesn't want to let her understand a man.
It seems that Self is ultimately, intimately unknowable.
What a lot of courage does for someone who is completely demoralized!
A mind is a very complicated thing--You can't just step in there and wade around, as some psychiatrists would do.

Part I

I'm a complex nobody.
Today, I have to change my ideas against those of others, or, to
simply change my ideas.
My father, with his writing, was a word machine. My mother,
especially with the telephone, was a talking machine.
I can neither hear nor talk. I have no one to speak to me nor anyone
to talk with. This is what my isolation has brought.
I have my mind in my mouth.
Something has taken me over in this place. It isn't so much other
people as the mental illness.
How controlled I am, and how uncontrollable it all is.
Schizophrenia--the mind and the body don't fit into the world.
People aren't people. There are too many machines.
I don't like a lot of what I'm sensing. My senses are attuned to
nonsense.
I'd rather talk to myself than listen to myself.
I am colorful, humorous, lazy, energized, imaginative.
Insanity is the inability to think your thoughts the way you would
like to.
I can't do anything without being used by it.
Mine is a mind overthrown by noise.
I don't affect objects the way they affect me.

Part I

Almost complete lack of responsibility has rotted my brain and
body.
Sexual behavior is almost gone. I am without a partner. Occasional
masturbation. Sitting. Walking around in the nude at night. Desire
is pretty much gone.
No TV. No radio. Silence in the house--it is difficult to hear it.
I have stopped reading.
Exercise has become essential--walking, bicycling.
I go to bed around 7:00 PM.
I go through the day with one hand tied behind my back.
With the onset of old age comes the death of testosterone, the
disappearance of hostility, aggression, sex, longing and desire.
I am unable to stop blanketing the world with ideas of reference.
Most of my consciousness is inappropriate for someone like me,
someone of my age.
Gonna missed the boat.

Part I

The nudity has gone to my head.
Too many unanswered questions.
My mind had become so weak that I am having difficulty
conceptualizing. Instead, I have to talk aloud to myself.
I have become very lazy and fearful.
No matter how long I contemplate myself in the mirror, I can't see
myself. Without it, it is equally as bad.
Sexually I was too late. Sex was a major component in the
emergence of this new illness.
My relationship with Nature has broadened and expanded.
I pass the time letting my thoughts stream past my inner eye.
They stream past, largely incomprehensible as if I were sleeping or
dreaming. I spend a lot of time each day doing this. I always have a
feeling of discomfort with the incomprehensibility.
The more the psychiatrists tinker with this illness, the worse it
gets.
The mind of an older person is different in some ways from that of
a younger person.
My whole picture of women has changed, e.g. nude photographs on
the Internet. I have not yet managed to accommodate this.
No longer dependent on the past, I live in the present.
Sinning deeply here in the Mount Holly area--in fact, every time I
turn around.
Wasting time has become more comfortable.

Part I

The radio, the TV, the computer talk for you. You don't have to
think. You don't have to say anything.
The effrontery of the New Jersey scene is enormous.
I'm not exactly fighting an insane mind. I'm living within it. The
steps I take against it are like fighting fire with fire.
I don't want to participate in my illness. By that I mean participate
with the symptoms.
The human body is hell on earth.
The trouble with a mind is that it forgets.
I find American society rigid and stratified. In my present state,
there's no opening for me.
One element of this new illness is the inability to distinguish
between myself and external reality--everything is one.
The insanity is vast. It is like a huge building. You add a room every
day. It's like constructing a mind out of books.
I have tons of material. I am expressing it all the time--all in the
present.
My existence is basically incomprehensible.
It's easy to reason, but it's difficult to reason correctly.
I don't understand anything anymore. I've finished with
understanding.
I am a victim of psychotherapy and a victim of the Internet.
I have the kind of mindset that doesn't revolve around other people.
Try understanding a psychosis when you are in one. You can't do it.
It has a mind of its own.
Man's state is unhappiness--frowning inwardly. A woman is happy.
No matter what he says to the contrary, man is controlled by his
environment.
I see things, but I don't see them.
The insanity is mysterious. It works for me, but it doesn't.
I will never commit to mental illness. It commits to me.
I'm listening to some sort of thought process that keeps me alive.

Part I

I'm building someone old up at the expense of someone new.
My morality--What seems okay at the time is not okay afterward.
Mine is a sick mind trying to heal a sick mind.
My emotions have been severely disrupted by my traffic on the
Internet--Michelle 7.com, etc.
I'm the straggler around here--the unhappy one.
Random associations for memory and voice.
I was supposed to be these: a lady's man; a womanizer; a rake; a
libertine; a lecher--an all around bad boy.
I don't see any point in ceaselessly doing things that have no
meaning.
Proving myself to <u>myself</u>, not to others. I see only myself. I feel
threatened by others.
After disentangling myself from the media (Radio, TV), I have a lot
of time.
The insanity is like a drug. You don't have to think.
I'm buying a high class, professional woman (Gonna) to be my
spiritual whore.
The cause and effect of a mentally ill person's mind are ridiculous.
I can't figure my illness out with my own mind. I need help.
Consciousness has many different faces.
The inequality of human bodies.

Part I

With no resources, and against impossible odds, I continue.
My life has been pretty much over for about three years. Now, I'm just thinking.
The entertainment industry is always hoodwinking the public somewhat.
I participate in other's badness to stay afloat.
After a hiatus of some months, I started again with Dr. Botzen . I will have to entertain her again.
My consciousness as I have known it has almost completely disappeared. Replacing it is this insane voice. I now have no claim on reality.
One insane maneuver is doing things I used to do without knowing that I'm doing them.
I love everyone I meet, but I don't meet anyone.
We don't know what we look like--paintings, photographs, movies, TV.--All these only give images--mirrors, other people. Nothing gives a true image.
The conscious mind is not in touch with the unconscious.
A great deterioration in my thinking since yesterday.
I can't get out from under time.
The Being the world yields me is ridiculous.
I should listen to something I can't hear anyway--my thinking.
Nihilism is the result of bad thinking.
How genuine is a person's subjectivity?
I'm just a solitary man. I have no use for anyone.

Part I

The insanity and the old age were unplanned for.
Nobody is telling me I'm mentally ill. I alone know it.
The most basic, elemental life, without stimuli is necessary.
Otherwise, I can't cope.
Whether thinking is sane or insane, it is still thinking.
The explosion of my sexuality is illicitly gained.
Being is hard to attain, but easy to disrupt.
The world is my hallucination.
When love dies, there's no recourse.
In my life, there's no prevailing point of view.
New Jersey excites me beyond measure. I can neither control the
excitement, manage it, or understand it.
This schizophrenia is all a major hell, My mind is in constant
turmoil.
My imagination wears me out. It's such an ordeal.
I'm always looking for a male role model--in life and in art.
Who is this man I have raised here in the Mount Holly area?
People we ask for advice tells us what we ought to do, not what we
can do.
You can laugh at anyone you want, but someone always gets the last
laugh.
People live like this all the time, but I haven't lived like anyone.
Words make things smaller.
This life is imperfect.
I felt a fear of a bull in a dream. I didn't know I could feel that
much fear without actually feeling it in real life.
Some blind truth is out there, waiting.
The air is heavier this century--more full of pollutants.
No one acknowledges me. I acknowledge everyone.
A man can't see beyond his own nose. A woman sees everything with
her emotions.
I have never seen such a rapid decline in a person as in me, with
personality, character, consciousness, body--all declining. I am lead
to believe I am destined for glory.
What it takes hours to learn, takes only a minute to dispatch.

Part I

These words are just sounds.
Since 9/11, I have been undergoing one big phantasmagoria.
Lacking desire, you can't do anything. You can only do what you know how to do.
I don't know why I have been left out in the cold this way. It's because people don't know me.
What I allow myself to think can be dangerous to me mentally, especially when I get into foreign territory.
I can never get enough of what I want from other people.
I have no perspective. I act as if the time I'm in is <u>the</u> time.
Children expect love from adults. When
it isn't there they turn inward.
My point of view is expressed to me, unbeknownst to me.
You can cause another person a great deal of pain just by being yourself.
My desire is a shadow of itself.
My bureaucratic stance has gotten to me-- for instance, hiding behind lawyers.
I don't see why I should be condemned to live out my days here.
It's a struggle to maintain my identity.
I have escaped from everyone but myself.
I have to put up with an inner voice that constantly points at me.
I'm tired of obeying myself.
I go on with my word games whether I'm mentally ill or not.
I am envious, prideful, selfish.
Make it better for yourself before they come.
My attitude--<u>I</u> am. Nothing else is.
I am so caught up in making a personality I can't see straight. But for whom?
The best thing for me would be to cut me in half. Put one-half of me in the sea, and the other half in the sky.
1. The lack of others; 2. The prolonged lack of others; 3. The lack of culture; 4. The lack of good food.
I am trying to have a mind. Mostly, it doesn't work. So, I give up.

Part I
My consciousness fits any situation--unhappily, however.
This work has been an attempt to put things into their proper
perspective.
I always want something I can't have.
I wilfully head in some direction. I have no idea where I'm going.
I am not spitirtual enough to understand many of the things I have
arrived at in my mind.
Definition of my boredom: my mind doesn't want to know anymore of
reality.
It is a matter of seeing what is there, not what I see.
Before I try to do something, I ask myself: "What is it going to do?"
You know--this is really nice, but it isn't too good.
This is all well and good, but it doesn't do anything.
This is all okay, but it isn't.
I really do appreciate this.
You know, this whole thing is ridiculous.
There's nothing you can do.
The insanity is another dimension to reality.
I saw the sudden disintegration of my personality into some lesser
person--an old man, an idiot.
How could I see someone so well, and have the person betray me?
(Gonna)
The insanity is like an enormous book, with the pages turning very
slowly, from day to day.
I can't believe the human mind's capacity for forgetting.
I develop my own point of view. Other people have their point of view,
which I do or do not have to take.
A man is his own best fool.
I don't play by society's rules, except where they pertain to me.
I'm alive, but not living.
There was no delineation between me and Gonna, no demarcation. I
never knew where I began and she left off.
I hate making choices in midstream.
I make a religion out of being a failure.
My insanity: I'm splintered, broken off, in pieces. They are brilliant
pieces, but nobody can relate to them.
21

Part I
The idea of my mind self-replicating itself each day has disappeared,
as is the idea of my mind knowing itself.
I have a lot of trouble saying the simplest words.
Woman don't want what _I_ want from them.
I wait all my life to find myself. Then, I'm lost.
A mind processes evanescent sounds and images. You can't get hold of
them--you can't get hold of listening, seeing.
I try to objectify after a psychosis hits. I find it difficult.
I'm talking to myself _about_ myself. It's a therapy on into eternity.
I know a hallucination when I see one.
I'm the most absurd character in the state of New Jersey.
I'm not really thinking. Whatever _is_ thinking, is not really thinking
either.
I do a lot of vainglorious dreaming.
I can't relate to anything--things, people, myself. They all seem so far
away.
Allusions to this, allusions to that--finally I end up alluding to myself. I
have nothing else to allude to.
Somehow, this mental illness went out the window, only to come back
through the door.
Understanding of anything at all _is_ possible, but it is limited.
To look outside of my head means very little.
I don't have the kind of thinking I used to have. I just don't have it
anymore.
With the familiarity there is in society today, nobody can do anything.
There's still somebody here, but there's not much of him left.
The Scorpio game is about sex and control. I don't win it, but I think
that way.
The character that is me sprang out of nowhere.
Now I'm a target for society.
Modern reality happens too fast for anyone to understand.
There's a reason to keep away from complete nonsense.
I'm unevenly matched. I go into the fray with my eyes closed. I come
out looking defeated.
I can never be entirely happy with anything--there's always something
in excess which wants me to follow it.
During the day, I'm in a state of awakened foolishness.
Day after day, I have the same problems. I have gotten tired of them.
I got rid of them. Now it's just day after day. There's no one playing
my game. No one.

Part I

I try to figure myself out. Am I all of a piece? I'm not.
My conscious mind has become the victim of my unconscious--for
instance--tactile hallucinations.
My mind reflects external reality.
I can't find good food. I don't have any interaction with other
humans. I don't meritoriously strive toward accomplishing some
goal. I'm wasting the human being that is me.
All things move on in the world without me.
What is it? I'm simply fooled by my own thinking.
Everything is a question, but everything is not an answer.
Nothing does anything. I might as well be a nihilist.
As far as my thought processes go: mixed in with all these other
people's, what a joke!
Is the insanity of some other person worse than my own? My own is
worse!
My mental illness is something logically unsound.
Without TV and Radio, I have all kinds of ways of amusing myself.
Time passes and I forget to remember.
I have gradually deteriorated in this house over the past 10 years
into something that is not there.
My psychosis isn't harmful to others. It's just erroneous.

Part I

I plan to go on living within this void until something or someone knows me.
It's hard to know the difference between sense impressions and hallucinations.
My mind's eye can see whatever object it's looking at from any angle whatsoever.
I call my sense impressions "distortions".
Now we are all victims of impersonal forces rather than of each other or of our leaders, such as--for instance, global warming.
I can't remember my mental processes throughout the day.
I act as if "I should" and "I could".
I always remember that which hurts me, not that which is pleasant.
Knowing is relative to the time and place in which it happens.
My consciousness could only know so much of itself, and then it stopped knowing itself(psychoanalysis).
I've been so censured by psychiatrists that I have ended up censoring myself.
Life is an ever-changing multifariousness.
My consciousness torments me endlessly.
A sex-starved nation such as ours can't survive without homosexuality.
Before you fall, consider what you are falling for.
I'll tell you what to say, but don't expect me to participate in it(coaching).
I'm partly sick and partly well. Some days I'm sick, and some days I'm well.
I had never thought of my intelligence as being that important until I came to this area. It has only served to alienate me from the people here.
I can't satisfy my sexual appetite. The sex drive is unfulfillable.
With women, I am left with nothing. I have to eat myself.
You know of the division of the cells, but do you know of the division of the selves?
The circles are ever diminishing. It is as if someone were playing one of those old records.
I'm headed in some direction, but I don't know where I am going. I have no final destination.
Nothing is permanent.

I thought I knew what I knew. I don't know it. I've known this for years.
Too much therapy with too many therapists has lead me to believe that I am the only entity that is.
I'm familiar with Gonna. She's formal with me.
I relinquish my lifelong body to old age. I'm left with my thinking.

Part I

I have a lot of courage to continue this way.
The voices tell me what I am thinking before I think it.
When I step into the crowd, my words start to sound different.
My body is not an inexhaustible tool of my mind.
I'm living here. I'm living an existence.
I knew something was coming along today. I didn't <u>get</u> it, but I <u>saw</u> it.
What seems desirable for a time becomes undesirable.
A mind, set on a certain track, will eventually go mad if its needs aren't met.
My thinking partakes of the general consciousness, but not exclusively. Maybe it <u>should</u> partake of it exclusively.
I refuse to understand certain things because I don't want to know them.
I don't know what's wrong with my therapy. I don't have a hold on what I want to do in there.
My social skills have dwindled down to nothing.
Nobody seems to know anything about me but the government.
Beliefs are subject to change.
Certain rules of my mind are unchangeable--Puritanism, for instance.
Anything I let into my mind during a day comes back at some point, usually later on during the day. It is usually unrecognizable. It's the unrecognizability I don't like.
It doesn't occur to me to seek out people or things anymore.
The computer is telling me things, but I don't know them.
I don't take up any part here, but I do have a part. I don't know what it is.
I don't have any idea what I'm doing in this house!
The passage of time obliterates anything happening.

Part I

Recent ongoing insanity: sex and loss of control; loss of reason; loss of
morals; loss of personality.
Gonna's therapy--Come in, sit down, start talking.
Enough insane thinking, and I begin to wonder if I have a head at all.
The thinking is all over the place.
The thinking is completely logical. I determine in advance what is to be
thought, and then I think it.
I used to have some meaning to my thinking that wasn't very good.
Now I don't have any.
My consciousness is not me. It's all broken up. I don't strain to
understand it anymore.
The total devastation of Jan's leaving, among other things, has left me
insane. My mother's dying had something to do with this, as well as
the divorce, and Bendy's leaving. These things all happened at more or
less the same time. Boredom, living in this area, and taking on Gonna
contributed to this as well. I'm an insane man now, <u>in the world</u>.
I've had enough time to live a life. I <u>have</u> lived it. I've had enough time
to think about it. I <u>have</u> thought about it.
Gonna is a negligent girl.
The schizophrenia is telling me things, and to give meaning to them.
Mr. Hersey is someone that doesn't exist in the minds of people in this
area. To himself, he's a simple someone with nowhere to go.
I take things into myself. After awhile, my mind has enough of them,
and I reject them.
Ideas are ideas. They don't appear as ideas. They appear as simple
thoughts.
Likewise, science hypothesizes truths and lets them go.
I'm sick of everything having to do with my mind. I don't want to use it
anymore.
I'm a victim of other people's activity.
I can't love. I am loved.
I am this: too much thinking did me in; too much sex drive did me in; too
much therapy did me in; too much solitude did me in; too many cigarettes
did me in.

I can't get it because I don't want it.
You can always draw analogies with something, make allusions and
associations to something. I think this is possible.
I don't mind the mental illness much. Still, it puts me at odds with other
people.
The more paranoid I get, the more paranoid the outer environment gets.

Part I

My mind had been made up of myself and other people. Now I'm
alone without others.
The schizophrenia is of the brain. The insanity is of the mind.
I have been driven to inaction by my thinking.
As for computers, they're trying to unleash the consciousness of
mankind upon itself. That will be something if they ever get around
to it.
Insanity is taking on too much--more than you can handle.
You are given to understand that you are expected to do things at
the time that is provided to you to do them in.
You can't say anything to her because she resents it, and she makes
you feel like a fool for having said anything.
I'm a reflection of what people are saying and doing in this area.
How high and dry I have been!
Words have the power to liquefy any situation. Just throw a few
words on any situation and it's gone.
Gonna and me--It's all a one-sided relationship--She won't come
around.
The case with me is that somebody always spoils me.

Part I

I would like to be part of the world, but I'm not. Failing that, I would like to be part of my world, but I'm not. I can't even think. I'm left without anything.
I have the sort of consciousness which does not lend itself to reality.
I had some sort of bad attack this evening--like an epileptic seizure. I had forgotten to take my medication.
Nothing seems to be permanent in this situation--no mood, no nothing. I lack a time perspective. I can't see myself.
I wonder what is happening from moment to moment. My mind is not big enough to encompass everything.
Am I just collecting on some dream of mine?
Am I looking through a prism when I look at other people?
At the end of my life, all I know is this therapeutic thinking, disguised in various forms.
I am both separated from my inner as well as my outer experience-- especially my inner. It amounts to a form of insanity.
I don't see any of my thinking self in my acting self.
I long time ago, something happened that didn't happen, and I went on.
In life, you get what you don't want if you're a loser.
Something else is in charge besides my illness.
Some changes I've gone through recently: 1. learning to build computers 2. satisfying my needs 3. bicycle epiphany 4. buying 3 cars 5. masturbation king 6. divorce 7. 4 housemaids 8. learning how to smoke 9. nudity 10. seeing with my imagination 11. women 12. cameras 13. money 14. cats 15. coming of age in New Jersey.

Part I

There's nothing there, behind the words, there's nothing.
I can't believe how fast aging has happened to me.
During the day, my thinking is mostly suspended .
Between external reality and internal reality, I would take the
former just to get away from the latter.
Yellow flowers appear to my mind's eye--more degraded yellow
flowers. More yellow flowers appear.
In my effort to reject everyone, I end up accepting everyone.
I have rejected objectivity.
Society is too tightly controlled.
In this country, there is always some problems with couples.   The
woman always wants to dominate the man.
Here in my body, there's plenty of sex, but there's not much left.
He can make a mountain out of a molehill, but it doesn't amount to a
hill of beans.
The trouble with living in the present is that it doesn't give you any
future.
The voices go on forever, discussing the most innocent things.
The greatest joy is playing music with another musician.
The pictures I see are mostly <u>not</u> impressions on my retina. If they
are, they have been transformed by my imagination and stored up, to
be revealed later. I should have been a painter.
Nothing is just itself.
I get only what they give me. I don't get what I want.
Man, suffering from his own limitations, can't survive on his own.
When I'm alone, I gradually give up.
All mind is an illusion.
I became bored with my therapist. I started talking to myself in
front of a mirror.
This grand plan has some author, although it is hard to discern who it
is.
I've been here in life too long. I've learned too much. I can't
communicate much of it.
In this area, people are working all day. There's nothing else.
My daughter Jan loved to love people, but she didn't love herself.

Part I

I have been made an example of by society to show that I am
worthless.
A psychosis makes a person blind to himself and to reality.
I must constantly defend myself from the noise around here.
When we are young, our understanding is incomplete.
What strange characters my mind will turn out!
The conscious, reasoning mind can't find the answers to my
problems. Reasoning is not going to solve them. Maybe the answer
is silence.
In our society, I see myself as a non-functioning male, without work,
and with very few resources.
Reality is sad, dirty and ugly.

Part I

I couldn't make it there today. I had to catch up at night.
Today, my thinking originates in noise.
Living this way has been, and continues to be, the next best thing
to suicide.
These past 4 years, I have refused a lot of my inner experience.
For me, reality is an empty, sleep-laden hallucination.
I say my lack of feelings is my mind encompassing all things.
How am I going to live in the world? This question has been here
ever since my 20th year.
My mind is an associative factory. Names are an associative factor.
One name leads to another name, finally leading to no name.
The thick fatness and greasiness of it all.
I have the mind of an artist, without the creative impulse.
Always, with Gonna and me, the basic antipathy of an older man
toward an older woman.
I make up reality as I go on. This is prohibitive. There is a reality,
but I don't want it.
I can't do anything with a psychiatrist. I'm required to be my own
patient.
Self is an intricate labyrinth, leading nowhere.

Part I

This therapy, Gonna, this kind of thing, could fool anyone.
Mine is an original consciousness surviving as itself.
Association is supposed to lead to reasoning, not more association.
It still talks, no matter what its inside is like.
I repeat endlessly what anyone said or says until I am dead.
Too much freedom is not good for anyone.
I know why I'm such a success, but nobody else does.
I don't seek myself out on the Internet. I'm looking for information
that would lead me to someone.
A shifting point of view like mine is dangerous.
When my desire for someone dies, it is impossible to resurrect it.
Instead of thoughts---representations of ideas.
I use a computer impersonally, without instruction. I have been
looking for a person on the Internet--a real live person, not just
someone in cyberspace.
What I am offered in this area is a mixture of stupidity and
politeness.
I have an irrational approach to life.
Some of my negative feelings are absurdity, ridicule, humiliation,
embarrassment, shame, anxiety, disgust, anger, depression,
resentment.
My mind thinks more slowly than my computer. It is producing
women. I want to dominate it.
My spirituality, my talents, my gifts have all gone up in smoke, gone
down the drain. My sexuality, too, is gone, wasted. My mind is all
that's left.
The poor are guilty of not being rich. The rich are guilty of not
being poor. The middle class should be without guilt.

Part I

The selves of people I confront in society are empty selves. They
haven't explored themselves as I have. This makes it impossible for
me to relate to them the way I would like to. I can wonder about
them, but I can't go anywhere with them.
I have tapped into my libido with earlier experiences with a certain
woman.
Also, my experience with a certain psychoanalyst has opened my
mind to an illimitable space. Consciousness is all.
With a computer, you have the power to do anything at all with your
mind. Your mind isn't anything.
I feel I'm being seduced by everything. It's all a big trick.
I have no recourse here. This is a major theme of my life here in
this area.
I'm not making any demands on people. They're making demands on
me to conform.
Psychiatrists are very careful with their stuff-the spoken stuff.
They don't go anywhere with it.
I'm so pretentious. I'm trying to be perfect.
Life for me is unlearning, not learning.
With all its vices, New Jersey is one step above Nevada.
The belief in psychoanalysis is that you can dispel any evil just by
talking about it.

We're sworn to silence. We're living the magic.
Gonna is happy. I am envious of this. I want to destroy her
happiness, but I am unable to do it.
Will nothing ever happen?
I got old this morning (4:30am) taking a bath.

Part I
These notes are becoming washed out.
The act of hearing I call "active engagement".
I can't do anything with authority.
Words are unwieldy.
In the official lines of conduct--dealing with society--everything is
okay, but I have a big problem in everyday living at home. After 16
years here, I am just now getting food good enough to eat.
I'm afraid of homosexuality. I don't go near it.
Although I am once removed from this schizophrenia by having
doctors to treat it, I am still their victim and a victim of the
pharmaceutical companies.
There seems to be a gap between my experiencing of situations, and
my possible experiencing them. I am missing something.
I represent the world to myself, but I can't see it. I only see the
representation of it.
In my local neighborhood in this area, there's no basis for reality.
I call what I have been doing with my mind the past 5 years
"internalizing psychoanalysis".
I live in my existence every day, but thinking is dead.
Today it is possible to know anything at all. It doesn't matter to me
what I know.
Other people all give false messages.
People's faces are masks for consciousness.
All the misguided attempts to steer me toward some truth I shuck
off. I pay heavily too.
Sexual feelings are supposed to be attached to some object or
person outside oneself.
I have a difficult time leaving any situation I get into.
I am forced to lie about everything here. There's no freedom.
Everything seems to be preprogrammed. It seems to come at a time
when I'm not prepared for it.
Real and/or imagined slight leads to paranoia, followed by psychosis.
A person who laughs is safe to approach.
I want to destroy what I don't understand. Anyone would.
I never am. Something is always in the process of defining me.
Though meaning is everywhere in my world, I can never take it.

Part I
I have no idea of my own reality. People aren't giving it to me. I can't buy it. All I can do is speak it.
I'm a changing entity on psychotropic drugs.
The Martin Hersey-Gonna Botzen phenomenon--Neither one of them wants to give of themselves to the other.
Just as I have rancor toward society, so society has rancor toward me.
I'm in some sort of dazed, dreamlike state here in New Jersey.
The body is a gross enormity next to the mind.
At 65, I am in the process of acknowledging my sexuality.
The truth is that wherein is found the most meaning.
The present continually justifies the past.
Corporations act like people, but there isn't anyone.
I don't like going out in public anymore. I feel I'm getting ripped apart.
I didn't exactly walk here, you know.
The ideal therapy for me would be reconstructing my childhood.
I damn myself by my mistakes.
My daily experience is like that of a blind man having had his eyes opened and then closed, retreating into blindness again.
I have a myriad of selves, but not one is true.
I'm leading a charmed life in a fool's paradise.
I don't know how to listen to music anymore.
The voices put everything into words which is beyond my conscious awareness.
There's not always a full moon. There's almost always a full sun.
A man without a woman is nothing. A man with a bad woman is less than nothing.
Becoming is a long, laborious process. Being is only a brief, shining moment.
This is like a dialogue with nobody.
I'm playing to stay afloat here. I'm not doing anything with anyone at all.
I can't hold any image in my mind. This is one of the things that is bothering me; whence my taking photographs.
Nobody cares what I think I am doing. They're ready to get me.
There's always something ruling every moment of my life here.
The power of words to destroy imagination.
Mental illness confounds reason. There's no explaining it.

Part I
Gonna is a figurehead to me. I am older than she is. What can I do
with her?
It seems obvious to me that I have overreacted to something. I am
an old man who can't think clearly.
Failing sex, I converge on pictures.
I don't know where my thinking is taking me. There are other
people working to my disadvantage. I don't know what the point
of this is---people working to my disadvantage. I think they are
harming me.
I live here, halfheartedly.
I have nothing to do, (no job), and nobody to do it with.
Nobody knows me, but everybody thinks they do.
I have yet to discover what makes me leap out of bed so quickly
when I am with her--maybe getting a cigarette.
I was playing the game with Gonna unwillingly. She was playing it
willfully.
Jazz is the best music for me because it is nihilistic without
intending to be.
My idle mind produces Chimeras.
The truth might be in the speaker rather than in the listener.
The total unimportance of so many words.
The voice follows me like a shadow.
The wonder of the Age is that everyone knows everyone else.
I don't know what's hurting me. I'm hurting myself and I don't know
how.
I don't become aware of some things. I don't worry about them. I
belong to them. They're saying something, but I don't know what it
is.
They create the Hell and I live in it.
When I get something, I want to have it. I don't want it to
disappear. Everything disappears around here.
Whores are more insistent than other women.
I find I don't want what I think I want. My mind has a way of
tricking me.
My search for an American staple came to rest with the apple.
The words stop when I go to sleep.
I'm an absurd character that comes from nowhere.
Not how did I die, but how did I live?
Hardly anything is driving my thinking anymore. I can't have my life
revolving around food--eating and drinking.

Part I

My mental illness is designed to deceive me. It does a good job of it
too.
The names go round and round. It's all a big lie.
Reporting into nobody each day.
My life-my daily living-is like a huge wheel turning and stopping.
With computers, electronics has insinuated itself insidiously into the
mind of modern man.
I don't want any more of this. I'm tired of defending myself from
things that are invisible.
I can't be constantly referring to others.
I oppose anything that opposes me for a while, then I give up.
This is what it has come down to in our modern age: no man likes
another man as much as he likes himself.
I have been an unwilling witness of my mental experience.
A man is nothing to himself who can't see himself clearly.
No amount of reasoning is going to solve my mental problems.
The end of thinking is no thinking. I'm not listening to anything.
I'm sick of thinking.
I mindfully repeat each day.
The association with nude photography is with the image not with
the person.
I don't know who I'm talking to and they aren't talking to me.
This is all a dalliance with myself.
I judge myself. People judge me and I judge myself according to how
I am judged.
Mornings now are a drugged hypnagogia.
Women are the great levelers.
I have Gonna there in her office, but she doesn't do anything with me.
I'm completely isolated here in this the most densely populated state
in the Union.
I refuse to do certain things because there hasn't been anyone.
I no longer have much experience of life. I only go out in my car to
buy things and then go back to the house.

Part I

As my self-understanding increases, my understanding of others
also increases.
My mind does not see emotions.
I enjoy being in love and the lover, but not the lovemaking.
My mind is not constructed in such a way to help me. It leads me
downward toward destruction.
I'm a vessel for ideas I don't understand.
I've had enough of everything in this house. I could last for a billion
years this way.
I am always distancing myself from my experience.
I create unnecessary situations that I get bound up in. I don't know
why. I'm not free.
The forces that are at work in today's society are too strange for
anyone to understand.
You can do practically anything today, but not everybody does
something.
Cosmic consciousness is knowing everything and loving everyone.
I can't get enough love, but I can't give any love.
No one acknowledges me. I acknowledge everyone.
A man can't see beyond his own nose. A woman sees everything with
her feelings.
I have never seen such a rapid decline in a person as in me, with
personality, character, body and body image, consciousness--leading
me to believe I am destined for glory.
I don't have the least suspicion anything is happening around me.
What it takes hours to learn takes only a minute to dispatch.

Part I

With the degeneration of my eyesight and hearing, I have gone
inside with visions and voices which, when they are over, I remember
practically nothing.
My consciousness is not me.
Self-generating words.
Today my mind has been taken over by out of control, associative
reasoning.
I'm thinking on one level and insane on another.
I try to maintain my sanity in spite of my illness.
There's nothing to fill the void inside a human but words.
While I'm insane I don't have any feelings.
Instead of _hearing_ my internal voices, it's as if I were _thinking_ them.
Why not abandon everything without. It's all there anyway.
In this insanity, my point of view continually changes.
All of this is insanity: The person, the thinking, the behavior, etc., etc.
The best thing you can say about me is that I am a victim of
psychoanalysis.
The thinking is in primitive states. I am using words in special ways
that amount to insane episodes. Also, the music which accompanies
them is also in a primitive state.
That will be the day when I don't have to talk.
I'll be okay the day I can think my thoughts in public.
There is so much simultaneity in the world today you can't tell one
event from another.
I do not always act reasonably. I am not a reasonable man.
Man's thirst for knowledge is insatiable. He will go to any length just
to find one thing out.
I get self-conscious. I feel people are looking at me and talking about
me.
I have a lot of respect for other people, but not much for myself.
It seems as though 1+1=2. Unfortunately, for me, 1+1=1.
All this happens in my mind. Whether it actually happens is another
matter.
I'm beginning to think of intelligence as a curse.

My mind is strong enough now that I can watch television.
I can't differentiate myself from other people.
I thought maybe something I knew would be relevant to me.
I can't take a more despairing position. I am at the bottom. There's no more bottom than death.
I'm totally bewildered by my sense perceptions. I can't function.
I'm going to be embarrassed by someone, and then I'll embarrass myself.
I used to know the difference between one thing happening and another.
I forget that time has passed. I'm looking for Being in names and words.

Part II

The opportunities for speech for me in this area are few.
I don't know what comes into my mind anymore. I'm dependent on
other people.
My daytime insanity is the left side of the brain taking over,
producing a stream of words that is out of touch with reality.
I have a lot of defenses against myself, but none against other
people.
I pass these days without any purpose or goal.
I forget the steps I'm going to make. I don't really make them.
Old age in America is irresponsibility, being ostracized and left
alone.
It's not enough to have outer order. I must have inner order as
well.
None of my observings has any meaning. The observing _is_ the
meaning.
Here in this area, I'm addressing people who have no way of knowing
what I m talking about. It looks funny.
My actions with objects all had meaning at one time. Now the
meaning has withdrawn. Also, words have some meaning, but not
always, and their meaning is incommunicable.
It's embarrassing where your associations will take you.
If something isn't there when it's supposed to be, I forget it. I
don't care.
My absurdity is to speak to no one.
Something is waiting for something here, but I don't know what it is.
Desire is wanting something. If you get it, you don't want it
anymore. Or you don't get it and you're hurt.

Part II

Living like this is the penitence of my life.
I've been hidden away from people so long I can't see myself
anymore.
I have never had my reason so fully intact inside a delusional system
as I do now.
I'm trapped in here. My mind is going insane each day and there's is
little I can do about it.
I can think I'm doing something but, as to whether I am doing it or
not, that is to be decided.
Sometimes I don't have the will to continue. I don't want what I've
got.
There's no fixed consciousness--here--in me---no fixed way of
looking at things.
This thinking of mine is all contrived by someone who doesn't even
know.
The thinking is understandable, but I don't understand it.
I'm not saying any of this to anyone. They're letting me say this so
they can go on with things.
After words, what? More thinking...
My life is a repetitious, boring affair with nobody in it.
Worshipping women has got me into a lot of trouble, with myself and
with them.
Mentally, I don't like to intrude on other people. Physically, I don't
know.
My schizophrenia is a lot of thoughts leading nowhere. Even to
entertain this thought is painful.

Part II

I'm just an onlooker here.
This century has brought more sophisticated ugliness.
If I suffer more, I'll die sooner. I'll be out of this foolish
entrapment with this area I'm in.
I'm about five years too young.
The good will take care of the lesser.
It is much more difficult to see the moon than it is to see the sun.
I've thought myself out of existence. I'm dead.
Silence is the great fooler and the great foolmaker.
I'm in this for my own pleasure.
My unconscious continues to spew out the most outrageous sexual
images.
These things all needed to be said, but they didn't <u>get</u> said.

Part II

I'm aging much too fast. It's stress from living in this area.
You have to have a mind of your own to start out with. You can't
just join "the minds".
I find human beings to be much more complex than they seem. On
the surface of it, everybody's the same.
After 16 doctors, I'm still trying to understand myself: Ackerman,
Brady, Cotzen, Dooley, Farber, Feldstein, Furst, Glass, Green,
Hauben, Heydt, Mendelsohn, Oxenhorn, Ross, Thompson, Weber.
I can't believe that, at the end of my days, I am here in the Mt.
Holly area with nothing to do, knowing no one, with only a little
money, and nothing to buy but food and clothing, cigarettes and
computer parts.
Only the dead can walk in their skulls.
I have to be in a listening posture to hear these hallucinations.
I have the hardest time getting hungry now. There's nothing to
hunger after.
My contacts with the world are soon to be forgotten.
There's no reality to be dealt with in the house. There's no other
person.
The mystery of the age is that nobody knows anything of value.
There's very little to value except money.
I can't believe Gonna. She talks to me as if nothing had happened.
I have my integrity. I don't relinquish it.

Part II

I think my brain controls my body, my physical health.
This schizophrenia is a life-long adventure, with some very wrong
turns.
I live here, but barely.
Friday, Saturday, and Sunday leave me high and dry here in the
Mount Holly area.
I drive people away with my speech.
My understanding is ahead of my meaning.
I can't talk a voice out of talking to me, especially these inner voices
I have now.
For one thing, the insanity comes on because I have nothing to think
about.
I have been irritated by seeing my inner world these past five years.
The present is smaller than the past or the future.

Part II

I consider myself to be a finished product of society. There's
nothing left of me.
Today every man has his murderer.
For me, there's no future without fear--the future is an
unbridgeable gap.
Sometimes my thinking runs along concurrently with reality.
What _is_ my sexuality about or for? It's for pleasure.
There's something in me that doesn't want my spirituality.
I have an inner light animating me.
Most of the time, I don't pay attention to my illness. I let it go.
It's easy to see: I lose my reason, not my consciousness.
What am I doing? Is this project under my control, or just under
my observation?
My insane mind is a mind born out of boredom. It's like a machine
that goes on for hours.
People are good, but they are not _that_ good.

Part II

An important part of this psychosis is this insane music. This
strange, backward rhythm seems to be a reaction to my outer
environment. The melody is the rhythm. It seems to be rhythmic
thinking.
Hidden from me was this inner world I discovered when I was put
on psychiatric drugs.
I don't have anything more to do with women. I love them, but they
don't love me. They seem to me to be selfish. In this country, they
get more than they deserve.
My insane mind is like a detective following me down the street.
When it comes on, it rolls on like a steamroller.
Not enough time to think. I'm panicking, heading for the door.
Without someone, I can't do anything with the spoken word.
The thought processes of any given individual don't matter much.
Now I don't know my thoughts from my voices.

Part II

There are only words between me and reality.
My mind does not have the proper nourishment in this area.
I'm almost invisible to people.
As an older person, my perceptions are skewed.
The meaning isn't in things anymore. I can't make it happen either.
I can always pile meaning onto things that have no meaning.
I am getting more and more anxious as situations present
themselves to me each day.
All that is bolstering me up is this insanity. I don't have anything
else.
The insane doesn't mix with the sane. I think I can do it, but I
can't.
My mind reveals itself to me gradually.
I can't hear myself when I'm speaking to myself. It's not a matter
of the hearing, but more a matter of where the talk is going.
You can't communicate something that someone doesn't already
know.
My consciousness has become more and more complex. It is more a
misunderstanding than an understanding.
I've explored all channels to find myself. I haven't found an entity.
Hearing informs the sense of sight.
What is thinking for except communication?

Part II

You can't eat a hallucination. I have tried to.
I get attacks once and awhile. The area in my brain responsible for
keeping words in order, in orderly sentences, is attacked. I am left
with jumbled up phrases and almost total misunderstanding.
I'm comforting myself with words each day.
"Mind" is a word to describe a certain way of thinking.
I'm sinking more and more each day into a lethargy.
I've finally stopped complaining about having to wear concrete boots.
My mind is not very good. Things are not similar as I say they are.
My connections are too far reaching.
I'm a pastiche of people, things, and ideas.
As for men, their love of any woman is not true.

Part II

I must say, this illness has given me some strange perceptions.
In this, the 21st century, no man has the Truth.
Now that I have familiarized myself with my inner world, there's
nothing to worry about.
I am fighting an unseen enemy here.
My own activity is useless here. It produces more self.
My mind is always engaged with others who are not here.
It gets away from me. Words are so slippery.
Wittgenstein was not a philosopher. He was a semanticist.
I am always fighting between reason and unreason.
I am expressing thoughts to myself that I don't even have.
This is all in a manner of speaking, but it isn't anything I can use.

Part II

Computers have been a mind-expanding experience, but not as much as other people.
I don't have enough here to keep me busy. It's the end of me.
My enlightenment has been here for a long time. I don't know why it is taking so long to show up.
Substituting eastern superstitions for western ones, we have the New Age Movement.
There's no Martin here during the day; there's just a little gentleman.
I haven't been able to accept any plan or mode bigger than me here in New Jersey. I'm just a little person.
My insane mind has the same sort of structure as my sane mind, but its content is expressed differently.
Gonna is irritated with me. I don't think she knows what she is doing.
I am under some sort of spiritual torment, but I don't know what it is. I'm not listening to myself.
I try to eat my body figuratively. It produces pain.
I am discouraged living here. I want to move out of this area and out of this state.
The steps I have made regarding myself and other people have become useless to me because of my illness and because of the passage of time.
The simplicity of women's design.
Contradictions everywhere I look.

Part II

My importance to myself!
I'm a victim of my own misunderstandings.
Whatever is wrong with me is really wrong.
I'm having difficulty living, difficulty dying.
It's a constant struggle for an older person to maintain homeostasis.
I'm always heading for heaven.
Something is always impeding human relationships.
The intellectual is worth nothing in this country. This is a big
surprise to me.
My mind represents <u>itself</u> to me, not reality.
Water, water, everywhere and not a drop to drink. I would say this
about New Jersey.
I'm drifting into obsolescence.
If somebody hasn't thought of it, somebody else has.
The other people of the world want to be Americans. They don't
want to be Americanized.
I've come to respect these voices for what they are, not for their
content.
I can't use therapy in any aspect of my life except for itself.
I don't have any other reason to be here other than that I <u>am</u> here.
The more I speak, the less she listens. The more I speak, the less <u>I</u>
listen.
I don't have it for women anymore. Now they are simply obstacles
to my understanding.
The point is not understanding but doing.
The mind is appearance. The brain is purely physical.
My absurdity has to do with not knowing completely. It hasn't
much to do with other people.
My mind has a stubborn obduracy and willfulness. It refuses to see
anything. It goes on about its business.

Part II

Nothing is left unsaid here.
I'm trying to get words to dispel my symptoms.
I'm still acting sane as though there were people around me.
The voice of insanity reasons like that of a human being's, but makes
nonsense.
A woman will let a man take his place with her, but a man won't let a
woman do anything.
I find all this psychologizing I do with Donna embarrassing.
I'm not now entertaining any ideas of doing anything or being with
people in any way.
I live by certain rules I don't observe. They are rules made with
discernment and insight.
My acting comes too late after my reasoning.
It doesn't matter who <u>you</u> are. They want to tell you who <u>they</u> are.
I've been remiss about my inner world. It's in a safe and I've
forgotten the combination.
Things remain the same. My attitude toward them changes.
Gonna shows herself sometimes as my inferior, sometimes as my
superior and sometimes as my equal.
People don't want to talk to me. They've already talked to me.

Part II

My living here in this area is all a serious case of maladjustment.
The freedom of man is what? Nothing.
Without the church, modern man is indicted. He has been indicted
for at least 150 years.
The meaning is in the words, not in the person who hears them.
I can blame the people who live in this area for being there.
I always wish for the unattainable. It keeps hope alive.
When it's a question of another person, all my thinking dovetails into
that encounter.
Pleasures die.
I still don't have my reason. What I <u>do</u> have is some kind of
makeshift person.
The things which I decide to keep as my truths are changing from
day to day.
My awareness is selective.
This place is an idle retreat.
I know my reality is baseless. I don't have any basis for it.
Therapy has wrecked my thinking about myself and about other
people.
Somebody is always lying.
The insanity is engaging me in a way that I can't engage others. I
lose my objectivity.
Socrates was a wordman.
I'm not free to take liberties with language around here. People
speak one tongue and that's it.
I am free to decide whether I am experiencing a hallucination or
not.
What is the actual value of words today?

Part II

This isn't a mind at all. It's just something that thinks.
With these voices, such trivial nonsense is turned out.
Time moves too fast in this country.
My mind has certain rules that it follows, whether I like it or not.
My sense of hearing would lead me to believe I have a big delusional
system working off of the State of New Jersey.
The insanity is a reaction to the environment: the people, the
places, the things.
Something has taken over my consciousness entirely. I'm not aware
of what I'm doing when I'm alone. And I <u>have</u> been alone these past
five years. It is something I can't explain. I can't understand it.
The 21st century is a big, solid mass.
I try to justify my thinking with objects outside of myself.
Jesus was a mystic visionary who got in trouble with the Romans.
We are all implicated in his death.

Part II

I am not only what I am thinking I am, I am also what I am thinking
I am not.
My stubborn will is pushing me through these days.
There's either a lot of nothing or a lot of something that ends in
nothing.
Objects are not just objects to me. They are living beings.
Too much has come my way in too short a time.
Gonna is only mildly, benevolently interested in me.
Once humiliated, always humiliated.
After 45 years of therapy, there's no healing process going on in
here.
I have a lot of fun with people, but they don't understand me.
I call this time the time of the renunciation of my inner life. For
what? For other people?
The past and the future are logically impossible, but it doesn't
matter.
With everything mapped out as it is for us today, it's hard to do
anything original or new.
My voices don't indicate that they know me.
Paranoia for me is defaming someone who is not with me who is my
friend.

In this house, there's no recognition of anything. There's just a long spiel.

This century is going to overtake this country soon.

The voices I hear all day inside my mind are composed of the most rudimentary English.

I can't step much out of the forms of vocabulary and grammar without becoming nonsensical.

It's my unremitting existence, not good deeds that make my heart beat.

I don't know what to do with myself. It looks like I have to conform to some reality I don't like.

With Gonna it is a failure of a love relationship, failure of a friendship, and failure of a therapeutic relationship.

I don't remember these mental aberrations going on with me. They are fixed and timed to go off at certain times every day.

I might have been a slightly naive, slightly innocent fool who didn't understand what was being done to him by other people.

Listening to my speech, to my thinking, it seems as if there were an echo, as though everything was redundant.

This whole American civilization is going on empty.

Today's music is harmful to the body and the mind.

In this--the 21st century, when you're dead, you're really dead.

"Consciousness" must be a joke.

When I listen to myself, all I hear is people shouting at each other.

In sleep, I have the mind of Tom Bunk and a cartoon landscape starring Beavis.

You can't get your mind from a book or from another person.

In this society, I am a psychological misfit.

Part II

This living here seems to be some kind of a mental exercise for me.
Nothing ever comes true here. It's all my being and nothing else.
I gave myself over to lascivious pleasures. I don't know why.
I say everything and it comes out that I am nothing.
I don't know what to say to anyone. They don't want me to talk to
them.
I have no way of knowing what I am experiencing.
Objects have their reasons too.
I don't know myself anymore. Nor do I know who anyone else is
either.
This century doesn't know itself yet.
These daytime voices are all progressions from sanity to insanity.
My words--Your words: our reality.
This insane mind is a stronger, more powerful mind than my sane
mind, and--bigger.
My consciousness is not directing my behavior.

Part II

I'm making up a lot of auditory hallucinations to run my thoughts
through.
My whole belief system has come into question. I don't know
anything. Psychiatrists did this to me.
This insane voice is something inexorable.
Men are destructive. Women are creative.
I am not able to make emotional advances to anyone.
When I go out in public, I am reaching out to fewer and fewer
people.
I don't have any fear of anyone in particular. I'm just fearful.
I can't associate with a computer.

Part II

My glass is always half empty.
My work with psychiatrists has brought my wanting-desiring into question. I don't think there's any answer.
Whatever _is_ known should be _made_ known.
It's not just the loss of meaning in the world today, it's the profusion of nonsense.
My insanity offers me an innumerable number of things to think and ways to think them.
It's as if I've accepted this broken up consciousness as my own.
I have a gap between what I knew then and what I know now.
I'm a prisoner of my consciousness.
Some of my hallucinations seem to be misplacing of objects, people.
Who knows who is whose enemy today?

"Therefore, if I am sensible,
I shall put myself right first."
-C.G. Jung